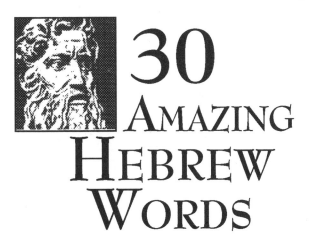

30 AMAZING HEBREW WORDS

Gregory A. Lint

World Library Press Inc.
Springfield, Missouri, U.S.A.

ISBN 1-884642-07-1

Published by World Library Press Inc.
2274 E. Sunshine
Springfield, Missouri 65804 U.S.A.

Introduction

Welcome to *30 Amazing Hebrew Words*. Soon you will discover how a few Hebrew words can revolutionize your Bible study. You will also better understand what you hear in sermons. And you will feel more confident when sharing your own knowledge of your relationship with God.

What Can This Book Do For You?

30 Amazing Hebrew Words is a fascinating and helpful study of the concepts which constantly interweave throughout the Old Testament. Every Bible lover needs to have a framework to build on to be able to adequately study the Bible. Scholars call this systematic theology.

With *30 Amazing Hebrew Words* you can discover fruitful insights to the Old Testament which will enhance your understanding of God's Word. While savoring these enriching word studies, you will be learning the basic concepts necessary to launch a life-time of enjoyable Bible study.

Who Benefits From This Book?

You will find that this book has valuable information for ministers and Bible students, as well as the average layman. As you unearth the concepts of the Old Testament you will quickly see why this book was named *30 Amazing Hebrew Words—Every Bible Lover Must Discover.* If you are a layman, *30 Amazing Hebrew Words* will give you information about the basic subjects in the Old Testament. An added benefit is that your personal Bible study will be enhanced as you begin to understand more about what the Old Testament writers thought about their times. *30 Amazing Hebrew Words* can also help you understand sermons better.

If you preach, but know little or no Hebrew, your sermons can take on new excitement with *30 Amazing Hebrew Words.* You can preach with confidence knowing that the information has been prepared with the utmost care. All information has been cross-checked by the most renowned sources of our time. In addition, you will be better equipped to step back in history, understand the thinking of the people of that time and bring an enriched interpretation forward in time to your congregation.

Knowledge Is Your Key To Empowerment

With *30 Amazing Hebrew Words* you will gain knowledge about one of history's most extraordinary languages. Many experts believe it was no accident that God chose Hebrew for the original language of the Old Testament. Hebrew is a particularly expressive language and its beauty can be understood and appreciated by everyone.

Some people might have you think that the average person cannot understand Hebrew words, or that a casual study of Hebrew will only mislead believers (or at best waste your time). The Hebrew word for this kind of thinking is "bologna!" Anything which helps you understand the Bible more fully is for everyone and is never a waste of time. You will find that questions will arise in your adventure of learning, but it will be worth the rich treasures you will uncover in the process.

Learning the Words

For each word which you will be learning, this is what to expect:

First you will see the word with a pronunciation key to help you say the word properly. Then you will discover the basic meanings. This will give you a background with which to begin. Most Hebrew words have several meanings with one being the most common definition. The first part of the definition section gives you an overview of the basic meanings of the word. Many key Old Testament words had one nuance in Hebrew writings which describe every day events, but took on new and powerful significance with the exciting writings of Moses, Samuel, the prophets and others. Some refer to these as "born-again" words.

You will then be given a helpful Old Testament study of the important concept this word conveys.

Significant Scriptures will be given and you will be challenged to look them up in whatever Bible study tools you use. You can begin your own exploration of the Scriptures with the information found in *30 Amazing Hebrew Words.*

Each discussion will conclude with a sample verse that highlights the meaning. The word being translated will be in bold print. These verses have been carefully chosen to bring out the main concept of the word being discussed. Many of these verses will be quite familiar to you and will inspire you to begin a new search of a favorite passage. You will find that these simple 30 words are the keys which will unlock an Old Testament scriptural understanding that you might never discover in any other way.

You should reread this book as often as you like to learn at your own pace. You may not be able to memorize every word the first time through, but this is common.

Knowledge Begins With the Turn of This Page

Now it is time to get started with *30 Amazing Hebrew Words.* May God bless you and illuminate your heart in your study.

Although there are many titles for God in the Bible, there is one name that was revealed to Moses at the burning bush (Exo. 3:12, 15) which is considered to be the proper name of God. Scholars have disputed for centuries as to the actual pronunciation. It seems, though, that *Yahweh* (Yah-way) is correct.

One reason for the confusion lies in the fact that centuries ago, monks would not say the word for fear God would punish them. This may seem odd at first, but the monks felt that people were too unholy to mouth the name of a completely holy God. It is certainly true that the name of God shouldn't be spoken thoughtlessly or vainly.

Another confusing factor is the pronunciation, Jehovah. This word was formed by inserting the vowels for *'Ădōnî* (Lord) in between the consonants for Yahweh. Jehovah is not a proper word at all. Jehovah was invented to allow the monks to say God's name without actually pronouncing it. Jehovah was first used in 1520 by a man named Galatinus. Even though the name *Yahweh* was not revealed until the Exodus time period, Moses uses the name in Genesis with *Elôhîm,* one of God's titles. *Yahweh Elôhîm* is often translated, "The LORD God" and stands for the one True God, Creator and Master of all.

Reading the account of Moses at the burning bush in Exodus 3 tells us that God told Moses to go to Egypt and tell Pharaoh to release the Israelites from slavery. Moses asked God, "Whom shall I say sent me?" God replied, "I Am that I Am." This was a declaration of God's all-powerful and eternally existent nature. "I am" communicates existence and is the central word of any language. *Yahweh* is the proper noun form of the Hebrew verb *hāyah*—the verb of being. The far surpassing greatness of God is therefore revealed by His very name.

It is not by coincidence, then, that Jesus tells John, who saw the vision of the things to come we now know as the Revelation of Jesus Christ, "I am the Alpha and the Omega, who is and who was and who is to come, the Almighty" (Revelation 1:8). It is hard to fathom, but God has existed for an eternity.

Our sample verse is from Exodus 3:14. *And God said to Moses, "I AM who I AM."*

#435

אֱלֹהִים

Ēlōhîm

(el-oh-HEEM)

The first name or title for God found in the Bible is *Ēlōhîm*. In fact, the first verse in the Bible contains the word *Ēlōhîm*. Genesis 1:1 states, "In the beginning, God created the heavens and the earth." Moses began this book as is done today—with the title. It was common in that time, however, to place the title of the book in the text of the first sentence. "In the beginning," therefore, is the actual title of Genesis, which we know today by its Septuagint, or Greek, name. "God" is the first to be mentioned in the Bible. This is quite fitting since the Bible is God's revelation of himself to humankind.

Ēlōhîm occurs over 2000 times in the Old Testament. One important fact to note is that *Ēlōhîm* is a plural Hebrew word. This does not mean there is more than one God, as some have mistakenly concluded. Rather, it gives an indication of the three Persons of the Trinity—the Father, Son and Holy Spirit. The three are distinct, yet one. This is the meaning and yet, at the same time, the mystery of the Godhead. So, in the first words of the Bible, it is apparent that even in God's written revelation, there are some elements we as humans do not fully understand.

The Old Testament often tells us of God's character through the use of *Ĕlōhîm*. In Deuteronomy 10:17, Moses is delivering a sermon to the Israelite nation. Here Moses reminds the people that *Ĕlōhîm* is not like the false Egyptian gods. This verse states, "The LORD your God is God of gods and Lord of lords, the great God, mighty and awesome." Moses is emphasizing in his sermon that God must be respected and obeyed. He is not like man-made gods (*ĕlōhîm* is also used for this inferior meaning).

The prophet Jeremiah also preaches that *Ĕlōhîm* is supreme, both in name and in power. Jeremiah 32:27 states, "I am the LORD, the God of all mankind. Is anything too hard for me?" The answer to the question is implied by the asking—an emphatic no.

The Psalms continually tell of the greatness of God and of His many miracles and steadfast love. Psalm 46:1 is just one of hundreds of deserving tributes to God. This Psalm begins, "God is our refuge and strength and an ever present help in trouble."

Our sample verse is from Jeremiah 10:10. *Yahweh is the true* **God**; *He is the living* **God** *and the Eternal King.*

13

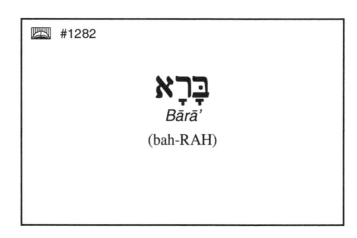

#1282

בָּרָא
Bārā'

(bah-RAH)

Bārā' means "to create" or "to make." This special Hebrew word is only used of God's creative work. *Bārā'* means to create out of nothing. Scholars sometimes use the Latin phrase *ex nihilo* to describe the truly creative power of God. When man "creates" or "makes" something, he molds, shapes, forms, cuts, etc. materials God produced. Genesis 1:1 tells us God created the heavens and the earth. *Bārā'* is therefore the first activity recorded in the Bible.

God is eternally existent with regard to the future and the past. At some "point," God brought the universe into existence, setting the planets in motion and creating time. St. Augustine philosophized that humans are in the "was" or the "will be," but only God "is," because He is not bound by time.

Ecclesiastes describes the search for wisdom, understanding and ultimately satisfaction. The only search that is ultimately not vain or useless is to "remember your Creator" (Ecc. 12:1).

Isaiah 43:1 speaks of God as the Creator of the nation of Israel. The Hebrew people came from Abraham whom God told to leave Ur of the Chaldees and go to a land He would show him. Abraham and his wife Sarah were biologically unable to have children because Sarah was past the age of childbearing. But God performed a miracle and Sarah did give birth to Isaac who later fathered Jacob who, in turn, fathered 12 sons. These 12 sons became the patriarchs of the 12 tribes of Israel which bear the names of Jacob's sons. Jacob was renamed Israel, which is, of course, the name of the Hebrew nation to this day.

While man can only rearrange what exists, God can still create out of nothing by speaking it into existence. God can even create a pure heart as David requests for himself in Psalm 51:12. God's creations are always good.

Our sample verse is from Genesis 1:1. *In the beginning, God* **created** *the heavens and the earth.*

15

Shāmayim is the usual word for "heavens." It is plural because the Hebrew language often expresses what is moving or flowing in the plural form. Just as today, "heaven" or "heavens" can refer to the sky, the atmosphere, the universe or God's throne. The Hebrews, as well as many other peoples, thought about the different levels above the earth.

In the creation account, God created the earth and the heavens above it. Genesis 1 views shāmayim as the atmospheric blanket around the new planet. The King James Version translates it "the firmament." Other translations say "vault" or "expanse." Each time shāmayim is used, it refers to some part of God's creation besides the earth and its contents. God's throne is also often referred to as shamayim (See I Kings 8:23, for example.)

In Genesis 22:17, God reaffirms His promise to Abraham that his descendants will be numerous and become a nation. God compared Abraham's posterity to the sand of the sea and the stars of the heavens. In this case, we know that "heavens" means outer space, but to the observer long ago in simpler times, what was known was only what could be seen by the naked eye. Shāmayim is therefore, in this case, "the sky." No one had any idea the stars visible on the earth are millions of miles away.

Psalm 89:29 recounts that King David was promised his family line would never be deposed from the throne as long as the heavens exist! The way this promise was ultimately fulfilled was in the person of Jesus, the King of Kings. The northern (and ironically much larger) portion of Israel saw many dynasties end in a bloody massacre. David's southern line, which presided over Jerusalem, never saw extinction, nor was any other lineage in possession of the throne. Jesus now reigns as prophet, priest and king forever established over the new kingdom—the Church.

Our sample verse is from Isaiah 66:1. *The LORD says,* **"Heaven** *is my throne."*

17

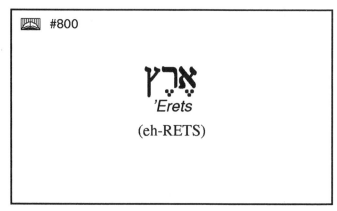

#800

אֶרֶץ

'Erets

(eh-RETS)

'Erets can be translated "earth," "land" or "ground." When Genesis 1:1 states that God created the heavens and the earth, the "earth" means the planet we live on as distinct from the rest of the universe. The interest of God in this relatively small planet is that humankind, the crown of his creation, inhabits it. That no other planet is mentioned specifically seems to indicate God did not populate other places.

Deuteronomy 5 contains a listing and description of the Ten Commandments. In verse 8, Moses is reminding the Israelites they are not to make an idol in the form of anything in the sky or anything on the earth. That is to say, not anything in all of creation. The principle being taught here is that we are to worship the Creator and not the creation.

Exodus 14:29 is an example of the word *'erets* meaning "ground." The Israelites, while escaping the land of Egypt, were surrounded by mountains on two sides, the Egyptian army behind and water ahead. God

parted the sea with such miraculous force that the Israelites walked across on dry ground. The ground
then became wet when the Egyptians tried to follow
as the sea closed again. *'Erets* is often used to mean the land that was
promised to Abraham and his posterity. Ezra was a
priest who also led a large group of Israelites out of
captivity, this time from the Babylonians. Appropri-
ately, Ezra repeated the warning of Moses from centuries before. He told the Israelites that the land which
they were about to enter was defiled because of the
impure way of those living there. He cautioned Israel
not to intermarry with the wicked or to make a treaty.
Only in this way could Israel be strong and eat the
produce of the land. Once again God gave Israel a
chance to be the nation of choice they were meant to
be.

Our sample verse is from Job 26:7. *He hangs the*
earth *on nothing.*

#7593

רוּחַ

Rûach

(ROO-ach)

Rûach usually means "spirit." It can mean the spirit of man or the Spirit of God. The first occurrence of *rûach* is in Genesis 1:2. Here the Bible states that the Spirit of God was hovering over the newly created waters as God was beginning the marvelous six days of creation.

An ordinary instance of *rûach* is found in Genesis 45:27 where Jacob's spirit is revived when he realized his son Joseph was still alive. Hosea 4:12 is a negative occurrence. The prophet Hosea warned Israel it was a spirit of prostitution which caused Israel to worship idols. Hosea was commanded to marry an unfaithful wife and often preached against the unfaithfulness of Israel to God, likening it to an adulterous marriage.

Most of the time, however, *rûach* refers to the Spirit of God. The Spirit of the LORD is placed on people sometimes to enable them to perform what God calls them to do. 1 Samuel 16:13 tells us that when

Samuel anointed David with oil, the Spirit of the LORD came upon the newly appointed king. Likewise, Joshua was endowed with the Spirit of wisdom when Moses laid his hands on him (Deut. 34:9). At the end of the Pentateuch (the five Books of Moses), Moses is about to die, and Joshua, who was the right-hand man, is appointed to take over as the new leader. Deuteronomy 34:10 then reports that no prophet ever surfaced like Moses, whom the LORD knew face to face. By this we know the Spirit of God "clothes" individuals in varying degrees, except for one.

In Isaiah 11:2, we read of the Messiah, the coming deliverer of Israel. Isaiah prophesied that the Spirit of the LORD would rest on the Savior (whom we now know is Jesus) without measure. The seven-fold Spirit of God remained with Jesus as evidenced by the descending of the dove at his baptism (Mark 1:9-11). Jesus continued to be enabled with the Spirit of the LORD, wisdom, understanding, counsel, power, knowledge and the fear of the LORD. This seven-fold Spirit anointed Jesus all of his earthly life and, of course, is with him before and after since the Trinity is inseparable. He was fully God as well as fully man.

Our sample verse is from Psalm 139:7, 8. *Where could I go away from your* **Spirit**? *Where could I flee from your presence. If I go up to the heavens, You are there, or if I make a bed in Sheol, behold, you are there.*

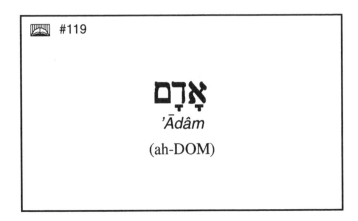

📖 #119

אָדָם

'Ādâm

(ah-DOM)

'Ādâm means "man," "humankind" or may refer to the first man–Adam, as in Genesis or 1 Chron. 1:1.

The first time *'ādâm* occurs is in Genesis 1:26. On the sixth day of creation, the Trinity consults and says, "Let us make humankind in our own image." Here the word means "humankind" because verse 27 goes on to say that this part of God's creation was in his image and that He created them male and female.

God is Spirit whereas man is flesh. 1 Samuel 15:29 distinguishes God from man. Samuel told King Saul that God doesn't lie or change his mind because He is not a man. Saul then stopped appealing to the LORD's decision for Saul to be removed from the kingship and began pleading with Samuel.

When Job's trouble came upon him, Eliphaz, who had come to visit Job, said "Man is born to trouble as surely as sparks fly upward [from a fire]." Eliphaz and Job's other two "friends" didn't give Job good advice or encouragement. When reading the Bible, we should remember some statements are not teachings, but simply records of what someone said. Unlike Job's advisors, the Book of Proverbs is sound advice. Proverbs 3:13 states that the one who finds wisdom is the one who gains understanding. This doesn't mean worldly wisdom that comes from humans, but the kind that comes from fearing the LORD. The fear, or respect, of the LORD is the starting point of true wisdom (Prov. 1:7). In return for reverence for the LORD, God helps humankind to fulfill his or her responsibilities and purposes on the earth. The Bible often teaches that some of the most important desires God has for people are to fellowship with others, care for the earth and, most importantly, worship God, the Creator of all.

Our sample verse is from Genesis 1:26, 27. *And God said, "Let us make **humankind** in our image, according to our likeness and they will rule over all the earth. And God created **humankind** in his image. In the image of God he created them, male and female He created them.*

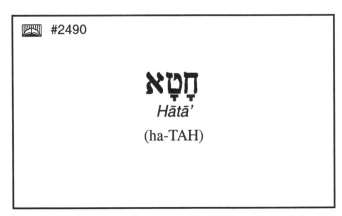

#2490

חָטָא

Hātā'

(ha-TAH)

Hātā' can mean "to miss" or "to be at fault," but most often means "to sin." The doctrine of sin is found in Genesis even though the Law of Moses had not yet been given. Adam and Eve sinned by disobeying God. This is a good definition of the word *hātā'*.

When Abraham went to Egypt because of famine, he told his wife Sarah to say she was his sister. Abimelech, king of Gerar, thought Sarah was eligible and took her for a wife. But before he could, God told Abimelech in a dream that Sarah was married. God kept Abimelech from sinning (Gen. 20:6).

Leviticus 5:17 gives an overall principle concerning sin and the Law which had been given through Moses. If a person sins, doing what is forbidden in any of the LORD's commands, even though he doesn't know it, he is guilty and will be held responsible. It's easy to see why it was impossible for the Israelites to stay clear of guilt for long. Sometimes sin can be against another person instead of against God.

In 1 Samuel 20, Jonathan is pleading with his father, King Saul for David, the king to be. Jonathan and David were friends, even though Jonathan knew David was anointed to be the next king and would dispossess Jonathan from the throne. Although Jonathan was in line to be king, he would not stoop to murder to preserve his inheritance. Jonathan boldly told Saul that it would be sinful to harm David, since David had only helped Saul (1 Sam. 20:4, 5).

The Word of God can keep us from sinning if we know it well. The psalmist said in Psalm 119:11, "Your Word have I hidden in my heart that I might not sin against you." God's laws are good, and designed to keep and protect.

God is a holy God. He wishes to have fellowship with humankind, but cannot tolerate sin. Sin, therefore, causes separation between God and people. If we confess our sins, He will forgive. In Old Testament times, many sacrifices had to be made to atone for sin until Jesus, the once-and-for-all sacrifice, came to give his life as a ransom (Mark 10:45). Even the Law, which was practically impossible to obey, and pronounced the guilt of sin on the world, pointed to Christ.

Our sample verse is from 1 Kings 8:46. *There is not a person who does not* **sin**.

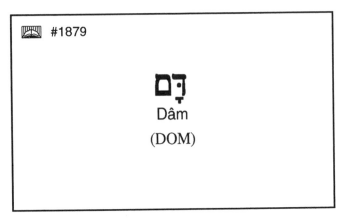

📖 #1879

דָּם

Dâm

(DOM)

Dâm means "blood." While the word may seem ordinary at first, it is the rich theology associated with blood that makes this word truly amazing.

God shed blood to make a covering for Adam and Eve after they had sinned. God told Cain that Abel's blood cried out from the ground for vengeance. God told Noah after the flood in Gen. 9:4-6, not to eat raw meat which still had the life-blood in it. Also, if anyone killed another, the victim's blood would be avenged because humans were made in God's image. This is the passage most often used to support a biblical view of the death penalty. These principles were related to Noah since he was the patriarch of the only family remaining after the flood. A new beginning was made and God wanted Noah and his family to understand and respect the theology of life-blood. God did not want a repeat of the Cain and Abel incident.

In the Law of Moses, this principle is repeated. Leviticus 17:14, 15 states that the life of the creature is the blood. It is disrespectful to God to eat blood. This is no doubt one reason why Satanists do so.

In Exodus 12:22, instruction is given to the Israelites to place the blood of the Passover lamb on their doorposts so the death angel would not strike the firstborn of their households. Blood sacrifices were the only way for the Israelites to acquire atonement of sin (Hebrews 2:2, 11:28). Millions of animals were sacrificed over the centuries in obedience to God's Law and as evidence of man's failure to save himself.

The same is true today. The blood of Jesus, the once-and-for-all sacrifice for sin, provides atonement for our sin if we confess our sin to God and profess Jesus as Lord (1 John 1:9; Romans 10:9, 10). The blood of the sacrifices of the Old Testament is the most striking example of the Old Testament pointing forward to the New Testament or covenant God offers to man.

Our sample verse is from Leviticus 4:6. *And the priest will dip his finger in the* **blood** *and sprinkle from the* **blood** *seven times before the LORD.*

בְּרִית

Bᵉrîth

(beh-REETH)

Bᵉrîth means "covenant" or "agreement." Covenants were important in Old Testament times. God made covenants with Israel and individuals, the most famous of which were with Abraham and David.

Because Abraham believed, God made Abraham's posterity into a great nation. In Genesis 15, after Abraham made a sacrifice to God, Abram (his name at the time) fell into a deep sleep. God told Abraham his descendants would be enslaved 400 years, but then they would come out with great wealth. In verse 18, God promised Canaan to his descendants--the land Abraham wandered in as a foreigner. This is an important part of Old Testament covenants, because the theology of land and blessing are closely tied.

One thousand years later, God made another covenant which built upon the first one made to Abraham. In another dramatic account, David is blessed by an irrevocable covenant promise.

David felt it was not right for him to live in a fine palace while God did not have a house at all. David told Nathan the prophet that a house should be built for God instead of the ark of the covenant remaining in a tent. God made a covenant with David in response to his desire to reverence God. Nathan told

David that although he wished to build a house for God, He would build a house (or rather, household) for David instead. God promised David his kingdom and household would endure forever (1 Sam. 7:11). Read this inspiring story in 2 Samuel 7.

David's covenant was based on God's everlasting love and his Word, making it secure (Isa. 55:13). Like the covenant God made with Abraham, the Davidic covenant further developed the plan of salvation through those who wished to please God.

Hosea 10:4 gives a description of the unsecure covenant of evil men. Israel, in the height of its sinful state, often made promises, false oaths and agreements that would not be kept. These vows are in direct contrast to the reliable Word of God.

Psalm 50:5 speaks concerning the sacrifices Israel made and the meaning of those sacrifices. In this Psalm, written by Asaph, God says, "Gather to Me my holy ones, who made a covenant with Me by sacrifice." The sacrifices and ceremonies made to God are not to be only a ritual, but a true expression of the heart. Today we can enter into a covenant agreement with God through the sacrifices of Jesus who died for our sins at Calvary. God will remove the penalty of death from us if we will confess our need and make Him Lord of our lives.

Our sample verse is from Exodus 2:24. *And God heard their groaning and God remembered his* **covenant** *with Abraham, Isaac and Jacob.*

29

> 📖 #2320
>
> זֶרַע
> *Zera'*
> (Ze-RAH)

Zera' means "seed" or "descendant." It often has the meaning of ordinary seed such as for planting. The common use can be found in Ecclesiastes 11:6. Here the preacher admonishes his listeners to work, sowing seed morning and evening to reap whatever benefits may come. Genesis 1:11 is another example of normal biological seed.

But there is a symbolic usage of *zera'* which makes this Hebrew word an amazing one. The first indication of the theology encapsulated by the word *zera'* is in Genesis 3:15, the first promise of the Messiah. In this passage, God is displeased with Adam and Eve because they had eaten of the forbidden fruit from the tree of the knowledge of good and evil. Yet, even in God's punishment comes promise of renewal. God tells the serpent who deceived Eve that there will be enmity between him and Eve, and between his offspring and Eve's descendants. Although snakes strike at the heel of man, wounding him, man crushes the serpent's head, destroying him. A particular descendant of Adam, Jesus would one day be struck by Satan as the angry mob was incited to shout, Crucify!" Although Jesus died, God had a purpose, and Christ rose again from the dead as victor over death and hell. Christ dealt the final blow in the dual and it was a deadly one.

Each chosen descendant of Adam passed on the seed through the centuries that would one day result in the births of Joseph and Mary, the earthly parents of Jesus. By miracle of the virgin birth, sometimes called the immaculate conception, Jesus was born. Noah, Abraham, David and many others were obedient to God and chosen to carry on the messianic line.

Isaiah is perhaps the most prolific writer concerning the Messiah. Isaiah 53:10 notes that, although it was the LORD's will for His Son, the Messiah, to suffer to atone for the sin of the world, He would see his offspring. This doesn't mean Jesus had any biological children, because He never married. Rather, the Church today is the result of the Messianic seed. Isaiah and Jeremiah both record the promise that there would always be a line for the promise of the seed to pass through. Jeremiah prophesied in 31:37, "The LORD says, 'Only if the heavens can be measured and the foundations of the earth below can be searched out will I reject **all** the descendants of Israel.'" Even man's sinfulness will not stop God's redemption of those who will be called by the name of the LORD.

Our sample verse is from Genesis 3:15. *And I will put enmity between you and the woman and between your* **seed** *and her* **seed**. *He will crush your head and you will bruise his heel.*

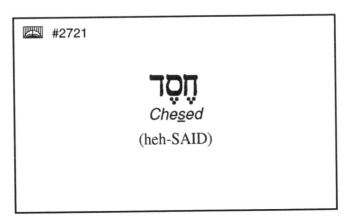

#2721

חֶסֶד

Chesed

(heh-SAID)

Chesed can mean "loyalty," "faithfulness," "steadfast love" and many other related concepts. The King James Version often translates this word as "lovingkindness" in the Psalms. When Abraham sent his oldest servant to find a wife for Isaac, the servant was thankful to the LORD for being faithful and reliable to make his journey a success (Gen. 24:27, 43).

Man can also be considered to have *chesed.* Nehemiah prayed that what he had accomplished by his faithful duty would not be destroyed (Neh. 13:14). Faithfulness and loyalty was also noted by Ruth's mother-in-law in the character of Boaz, the great grandfather of King David (Ruth 2:20). In 1 Samuel 20:8, David asked Jonathan to remain faithful to their friendship.

God's unfailing or steadfast love goes far beyond man's ability and is the subject of much Old Testament material, especially in the Psalms. Psalm 33:5

is a good example. Here the vastness or completeness of God's unfailing love is described as filling the whole earth, meaning God's reliability does not end. Verse 4 says that the Word of the LORD is faithful and true. The concept revealed through the word *chesed* emphasizes the unchanging good and holy character of God. In Exodus 34:6, God declares himself to be compassionate, gracious, slow to anger, abounding in love and abounding in faithfulness. This is the character of God wrapped up in the word *chesed*.

Our sample verse is from Psalm 115:1. *Not to us, LORD, not to us, but to your name be given glory because of your* **steadfast love**, *because of your reliability.*

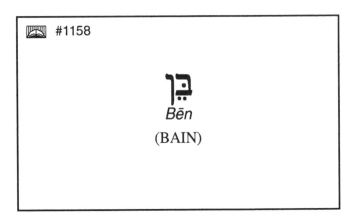

#1158

בֵּן

Bēn

(BAIN)

Bēn means "son" or "descendant." It is in many ways much like *zera'* for "seed" or "descendant." Both can mean "offspring" or "children." *Zera'*, however, is often futuristic, whereas *bēn* is realized. *Bēn*, therefore, as today, is a more endearing term, being a family member.

Genesis 5 is the first listing of genealogy in the Bible. Here, the ordinary sense of "son" occurs many times. In 5:4, there is a little more description given concerning Seth. The Bible notes that Adam fathered Seth and the son was in Adam's own likeness and in his own image. Compare this with verse 1, the introduction to Adam's genealogy where the creation of humankind is noted and that humankind was created in God's likeness. This lets us know that all people are in the image of God, the likeness being passed down through Adam and through each successive son. Collectively, Israel is called God's son (Hosea 11:1).

Hebrew has no word for grandson, so when such

a meaning needs to be expressed as in Jeremiah 27:7, it literally says, "the son of a son." In fact *bēn* by itself can mean grandson or simply descendant. It is even used of animals, such as in Leviticus 9:2 where *bēn* refers to a young calf.

A famous reference using *bēn* is Psalm 2:12. Here, *bēn* refers prophetically to the Son of God. Psalm 2 describes the supremacy of the Son as King of Kings. There is no good reason for kings to conspire if they are planning what God will not allow. "Kiss the Son" Psalm 2:12 states. This means every earthly king must pay homage to the true Ruler of the earth. All the political struggles of history will not prevent the rule of God's Son.

Our sample verse is from 2 Kings 10:30. *The LORD said to Jehu, "Because you have acted righteously in my eyes, the **sons** of four generations for you will sit on the throne of Israel."*

35

#6734

Pāchad

(Pah-COD)

Pāchad is a versatile Hebrew word with over a dozen possible meanings. Some of them are: "to make a search" (1 Sam. 14:17); "to take care of" (2 Kings 9:34); "to call to account" (Isaiah 10:12); "to appoint" (Gen. 39:4). Many Hebrew verbs are flexible. Some more important ones expand to several meanings. The King James Version often translates *pāchad* as "visit." Some other ordinary usages include numbering the people (Num. 1:3) or mustering forces (2 Chron. 23:14).

In Exodus 3:16, God told Moses to tell the elders of Israel that they have been "watched over" or "cared for" during the misery of bondage in Egypt. *Pāchad* is often used with God as the subject, indicating that He takes an interest in human affairs. But there's something more to this.

God intervenes in human affairs either to bless or to punish. In Amos 3:2, an example of God intervening with wrath can be seen. Because God was gracious to Israel by delivering them from Egypt and making them his people, their sins would all be punished because they, of all people, should have known better.

As mentioned above, when God "visits," as the King James Version puts it, it means God intervenes in human history either to bless or to judge. "Intervene" is a good translation in these cases. The first occurrence of *pāchad* in the Old Testament is found in Genesis 21:1.

God promised Abraham and Sarah they would have a child. This was not humanly possible because Sarah was past the age of childbearing. But Genesis 21:1 says that God intervened concerning Sarah and she became pregnant with Isaac. Some translations say God "was gracious to" or "blessed" Sarah. These renderings are also good according to the context. Sometimes the richness of meaning encompassed by a Hebrew word makes it difficult to fully explain by a single English word. We can be sure, however, that the concept of *pāchad* shows us God didn't just create the world and forget about it or us.

Our sample verse is from Genesis 50:24. *Joseph said to his brothers, "I am dying, but God will surely **intervene** concerning you and He will bring you up from this land to the land which he swore to Abraham, Isaac and Jacob.*

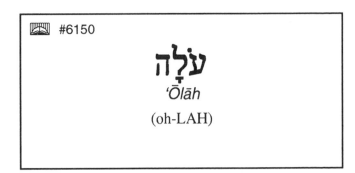

#6150

עֹלָה

'Ōlāh

(oh-LAH)

'Ōlāh means "burnt offering." It comes from the verb *'ālāh* which means to go up, so the literal meaning of *'ōlāh* is, "something going up." This refers to the smoke of the burnt offering and is thought of in this way because the offering is offered up to God. *'Ōlāh* can also refer to the animal which is offered as in Leviticus 1:4 and 5:7.

Many times in the Old Testament, people would offer a sacrifice on an altar to God at special events of their life to commemorate their commitment to God. Noah made an altar of thanksgiving after God saved Noah and his family from the flood. Of course, Noah obeyed God by building the ark and entering it, but this does not take away from God's grace to make a way of escape. After exiting the barge, Noah offered sacrifices to God from the clean animals and birds (Genesis 8:20). God was pleased and promised He would never again flood the earth.

2 Chronicles 29 tells the great story of King Hezekiah's purifying of the temple of the LORD. Sacrifices were brought throughout the days to be offered

to the LORD. All of the burnt offerings amounted to 3600 animals! This demonstrated the people's serious rededication to God.

Some wonder why there were so many animals killed in the Old Testament and why God would require such a thing as blood to be shed so often. Hebrews 2:2 has the answer to this question—"without the shedding of blood, there is no remission for sins." Until Jesus came and paid for the sins of the world, there couldn't be just one sacrifice. Every new sin had to be covered by new blood. The power of the blood of Jesus, though, is sufficient for all eternity because He is completely holy and death cannot hold Him.

More than sacrifices and burnt offerings, however, God requires a repentant heart and obedience. The prophet Micah poses the question in 6:6, 7, "Shall I come to [the LORD] with burnt offerings? Will the LORD be pleased with thousands of rams?" The reply is that God has shown us what is good and what is required. He wants justice, mercy and a walk of humbleness (Micah 6:8). Without these qualities, obeying even a God-given Law is useless. When sacrifices of any kind are made with true motives, however, God is pleased with the one offering.

Our sample verse is from 1 Samuel 7:9. *Then Samuel took a young lamb and made it go up as a whole* **burnt offering** *to the LORD. He called out to the LORD on account of Israel, and the LORD answered him.*

39

#1041

בַּיִת

Bayith

(bah-YEETH)

Bayith means "house" or "household." It can
mean the actual structure one lives in (Exo. 12:7; Judg.
11:3) or the family members who live under the roof
(Deut 6:22). It can even refer to a whole tribe. *Bayith*
can also refer to an estate (Gen. 15:2).

The most important physical house is the house
of God. In these cases *bayith* may be properly translated "temple" or "tabernacle." Judges 18:31 says that
the house of God rested in Shiloh in the time of Micah
(not the prophet).

Ezekiel saw a vision of a future temple, one that
would house the glory of God after this present world
passes away. Read Ezekiel 40 for an awesome description of the greatest *bayith* that will ever be con-
structed. God has had more than one dwelling place
among people. It began with the ark of the covenant
(which will be discussed later).

Solomon's temple was built after 1000 B.C.
Herod built the next temple which took over 40 years
to construct. About 40 years after that, it was destroyed

in 70 A.D. by the Romans. In 135 A.D., a war broke out between Israel and the Romans which caused the end of Israel as a nation. This condition remained until 1948 when the newly formed United Nations once again recognized the Hebrew state. Today, orthodox Jews are again seeking to build a house for God. Since the Jewish people did not accept Jesus as their Messiah, they still feel they need to offer sacrifices, but they don't have a place to do so. Many instruments which are patterned after the Old Testament instructions have reportedly now been made. The leading rabbi has even reported on Israeli television, the ark of the covenant has been found (although he also said it was too dangerous to recover it).

Perhaps the most dramatic passage containing the word *bayith* is 2 Samuel 7. King David told Nathan the prophet that a temple should be built for God, but God graciously said He would build a *bayith* for David. A double meaning is implied by God's statement. David already lived in a nice palace, so God did not mean "house," but "household." This play on words was the basis for the Davidic covenant in which God promised David his family would remain on the throne forever. This covenant was accomplished in Jesus. God wouldn't allow David to build a temple because he was a man of war, but God honored David's willingness to sacrifice and his worshipful attitude.

Our Sample verse is from 2 Samuel 7:11. *The LORD will build a* **household** *for you.*

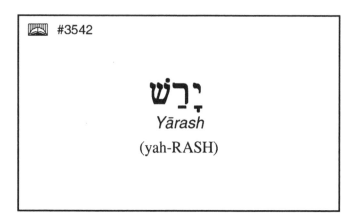

#3542

יָרַשׁ

Yārash

(yah-RASH)

Yārash is an important word because it is related to the promised land. *Yārash* means "to take possession of" or "to inherit." Throughout Israel's history, when they obeyed God, they took possession of land; when they disobeyed, they were dispossessed.

In Genesis 15:7, God reaffirmed to Abraham that he was called from the land of Ur to "take possession of" the land of Canaan. Eventually, the Israelites, under the direction of Joshua, took possession of the land driving out the Canaanites. (Unfortunately they did not drive them out completely and this attributed to Israel's downfall.) Before the campaign, Moses had cautioned the Israelites to remember to obey God's laws when they took over the land of Canaan so that it would be their inheritance forever (Deut. 11:31, 32).

Jeremiah often prophesied in a sarcastic way, taunting Israel into realizing they were living far below their potential. In Jer. 49:1, Jeremiah prophesies concerning the Ammonites, an enemy of Israel. The tribe of Gad was dispossessed. "Why?" Jeremiah asked. "Was it because Israel didn't have anyone to inherit the land from that tribe?" This obvious "no" answer was implied to Israel's shame.

Isaiah prophesied in chapter 61 that one day, God's plan will come to pass in fullness concerning his people. Isaiah 61:7 records that the people will receive a double portion instead of shame and disgrace, they will rejoice in their inheritance. The double portion refers to the share of the oldest son. If a man had four sons, for example, he would divide his wealth into five portions. The oldest son would receive two shares and the others one. God's plan is to give a good inheritance to his people. One day, a new heaven and a new earth will be given to all those who trust in the LORD. (See Revelation 21).

Our sample verse is from Genesis 28:4. *May He give the blessing of Abraham to you and to your seed for your* **taking possession of** *the land of your sojourning which God gave to Abraham.*

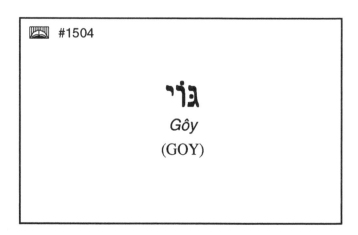

#1504

גּוֹי

Gôy

(GOY)

Gôy means "nation." It is often found in the plural form of *gôyim* which means the heathen nations. The concept of *gôy* is one of a group rather than a single person. It is then plural in concept being compared to *'ādâm* or *'enôsh* which both refer to one.

One unusual usage of *gôy* is in reference to a swarm of locusts, picturing them as an invading nation marching into battle (Joel 1:6). The impending judgment was due to Israel's sinful condition. The Bible tells us that Israel was God's chosen people. Psalm 33:12 records the fact that Israel was blessed because Yahweh was their God. He chose them for his inheritance. Isaiah 1:4 notes the sad state of Israel when they had forsaken the LORD. They had become so sinful that they are pictured as a sick person in whom no part of the body is healthy. Never, though, was Israel ever wiped out completely. One day, during the Great Tribulation, many Jews will realize Jesus is the Messiah and a righteous nation of Israel will rise again.

Abraham, as mentioned before, was made into a great nation. This promise is repeated several times. The first is in Genesis 12:2. By the time Israel spent 400 years in Egypt, they had grown to a population of up to 2 million. In 1500 B.C., this was a large number. Some try to dispute this by saying that the census numbers recorded in the Bible are not actual numbers, but symbols. The Bible should be interpreted literally, unless there is specific indication otherwise. It is certainly obvious the census numbers are rounded, but there is not founded reason to believe the count was exaggerated or some odd kind of notation. During the times Israel followed God, they were truly a great nation.

Our sample verse is from Zephaniah 2:9. *The remnant of my people will plunder them and those left over from my **nation** will dispossess them.*

Pe**s**ach means "passover." It can refer to the festival or the sacrificial paschal lamb. The Passover was instituted by God on the night Israel would be delivered from Egyptian bondage. They had been slaves to Egypt for nearly 400 years. Moses was sent to lead the people from Egypt, and ultimately, to the promised land.

The method God chose for punishment of Egypt was ten plagues, each one designed to belittle one of the false gods of the Egyptians, and each one increasing in severity. The first plague was turning the Nile into blood and the last was the death of every first-born male from poor man's cattle to Pharaoh's son. The importance of the plagues were not only to punish Egypt for their cruelty to the Israelites, but to show Israel that Yahweh is not a man-made god, but the God of the universe.

The first Passover night was to be observed on

the night the death angel would come. Only if the Israelites put the blood of the lamb on their doorposts, would the death angel pass over their households. As God struck Egypt, Israel escaped. That Passover night was to be observed every year by Israel and its meaning explained to posterity. It was the night Israel was brought forth as a nation to go forth in the name of the LORD. It was celebrated on the 14th of the first month (Lev. 23:5). If anyone was ceremonially unclean at that time, he could observe it on the 14th day of the second month (Num. 9:10, 2 Chron. 30:15).

The last meal Jesus had with his disciples before the resurrection was the celebration of the feast day of the Passover. The next day, Jesus would sacrifice himself as the Lamb for the sins of the world (John 1:29, 1 Cor. 5:7). Some wonder why Jesus did not die on the Day of Atonement. Mark 10:45 tells us that Jesus' mission was to be a servant and to give his life as a ransom–the one sacrifice for all time. Revelation 19:9 tells us that all Jesus' followers will have another meal with him celebrating the final victory over sin.

Our sample verse is from Exodus 12:27. *And tell them it is the* **Passover** *sacrifice to the* LORD *who passed over the houses of the children of Israel.*

The main meaning of *tôrāh* is "law" and usually refers to the Law of Moses. It could also refer to the teaching of a person, such as Asaph (Ps. 78:1). The Old Testament is divided into three parts--the Law, the Prophets and the Writings. So it's easy to see that *tôrāh* is an amazing Hebrew word. *Tôrāh* can also mean "instruction" or "direction." The word *tôrāh* comes from the verb *yārah* which means "to teach."

The Law was given for the purpose of guiding the Israelites in everyday life and to keep them holy by purification. Although it could point them to God, it could not give lasting redemption from sin. Nonetheless, the Law was good. Paul discusses the importance of the Law in the Book of Romans. He notes that trying to be holy according to the Law was totally frustrating and only through Jesus could anyone be free from the guilt the Law pronounced on the world.

The Psalms often speak of meditating on the Law of God and emphasize its goodness. Psalm 119 is the greatest of these Psalms. Here, the psalmist speaks of delighting in God's Law and how it guides us. The Law was so extensive, it took 40 days for Moses to receive it (along with the instructions for building the tabernacle).

Isaiah notes in 24:5 of his Book, that the earth is defiled by its people when they disobey the laws of God. God considers disobedience to be sin and He must punish all sin which does not come under the cleansing power of the blood of Jesus. The Law could not justify man, because we are justified by faith. The Law was given as a bridge until Jesus the Messiah came. The Law led to Christ. See Galatians 3 for Paul's famous explanation of the purpose of the Law. Pointing forward to Calvary, the Law made temporary provisions for the atonement of specific sins, but only Jesus could make provision for all sin.

Our sample verse is from Psalm 119:1. *Blessed are those whose way is upright; those who walk according to the* **Law** *of the LORD.*

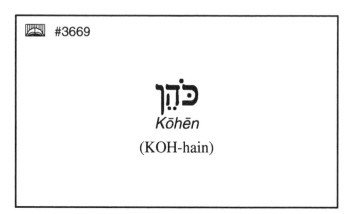

#3669

כֹּהֵן
Kōhēn
(KOH-hain)

Kōhēn means "priest." The priestly office was one of the three most important roles. The other two were the king and the prophet. Special persons in the Old Testament functioned in more that one role. Melchizedek was king of Salem and a priest (Gen. 14:18). Rare individuals, such as Samuel, fulfilled all three at various times throughout his ministry. Today, Jesus functions as all three being the fulfillment of all Israel.

Priests of Israel's Old Testament times, were of the seed of Aaron and were therefore all Levites, except on rare occasions. The Bible always makes mention of these exceptions. (See Lev. 1:5, 8, 11.) The priests performed all the duties of the tabernacle. Each family had a specific duty. Some transported the tabernacle; some cared for the equipment; and some sacrificed, etc. Only the high priest made the most important sacrifices, however. He entered the most holy place of the tabernacle where the ark of the covenant rested one day a year to atone for the sins of Israel. Joshua 4 records the momentous occasion of the priests carrying the ark of the covenant across the Jordan River into the promised land.

Isaiah 6:2 and 2 Kings 10:19 refer to priests of a foreign god. It is interesting to note that even pagan peoples of that time realized their need for direction and atonement for sin. During a time of rebellion, Jeroboam, the king of God's people, even appointed priests of two idols--the golden calves at Dan and Bethel. This was one of the most insolent acts against the LORD in Israel's history.

When Israel is restored in the end time, God will once again appoint priests for the new temple (Isa. 66:21). Offerings will be made, not for sin, but in thanksgiving to the LORD.

Our sample verse is from Joshua 6:4. *And seven* **priests** *will carry seven trumpets proceeding along in front of the ark.*

#751

אֲרוֹן

'Ărôn

(ah-RONE)

'Ărôn means "ark" or "chest." It does not refer to the ark Noah built to escape the flood. It usually refers to the ark of the covenant, sometimes called the ark of testimony. It can, however, have a more ordinary meaning. 2 Chronicles 24:8, 10, 11 refers to a chest that was made by command of King Joash. Money was collected in it to fund the restoration of the temple.

The majority of instances in which 'ărôn is found refers to the ark which was placed in the most holy place of the tabernacle. Here God's presence and glory was evidenced among the people of Israel. Read Exodus 25:10-22 for a description of the ark. This passage gives the detailed instructions communicated to Moses for the making of the ark. The construction was a beautiful work of art. Moses ordered the ark of the covenant made exactly according to God's instructions (Deut. 10:3).

There were three items placed in the ark. At the time of its construction, the Ten Commandments were placed in it. This was the covenant between God and Israel (Deut. 10:5). Later, a jar of manna was placed in it to remind Israel of God's provision. Finally, Aaron's rod was placed in the ark of the covenant to remind Israel that Moses and Aaron were appointed by God to lead the people and that rebelling against God's leader would result in punishment because they were representing God.

From the construction of the ark of the covenant, until the time Israel entered Canaan, specific instruction had to be followed in the caring for and the moving of the ark of the covenant. Joshua 3:6ff. records the great historic crossing of the river Jordan. The priests, following the strict guidelines, transported the ark to the promised land. The ark was also carried into battle. Later, when the territory of Israel had been expanded, a temple was built by Solomon to house the ark. David, Solomon's father, felt the ark should have a permanent dwelling place rather than the tabernacle, elaborate as it was. Israel learned, at the cost of lives in military combat, the ark was not a magical charm which ensured victory and blessing. It was only because Israel obeyed God and followed the commands of the LORD that his presence would dwell among and help Israel.

Our sample verse is from Exodus 25:22. *And I will meet with you there and I will speak with you above the cover between the two cherubim which is on the* **ark**.

53

#3848

כָּפַר

Kāphar

(kah-PHAR)

Kāphar often means what it sounds like, "to cover," but its more important meaning is "to atone." Sometimes men would give gifts to cover for their offense such as Jacob gave to Esau (Gen. 32). But the most important references are to the atonement of sin, bringing him into right relationship with God. One day a year, Aaron (and each successive high priest) made atonement for sins on the altar of incense (Exodus 30:10).

Atonement was a privilege given only to Israelites. People from other nations could become an Israelite, but this was rare, relatively speaking. Isaiah describes the fall of Babylon in chapter 47 of his Book. In 47:11, 12, the prophet records that disaster will come upon the sinful nation and no magic spell or ransom will make atonement enough to rescue them from God's wrath. How thankful Israel should have been for God's special provision. How thankful also we should be today for the provision of atonement provided at the cross. It was the duty of the priests to make atonement sacrifices for the Israelites. Even if the community sinned unintentionally, atonement had to be made (Lev. 4:20). The sin offering and the guilt offering were the provisions for the priests who performed the sacrifices (Lev. 7:7). This was one of the ways the priests got paid so they could provide for themselves and their families, because they did not get a land inheritance like the other tribes.

On the Day of Atonement, once a year, a goat was used to make atonement for Israel. The high priest would confess the sins of the people over the goat and then it was sent into the wilderness to die.

The many sacrifices were important for two reasons. They demonstrated God's great mercy to Israel (Ps. 78:38), and they pointed forward to Jesus.

Our sample verse is from Leviticus 16:32. *And the anointed priest will* **make atonement.**

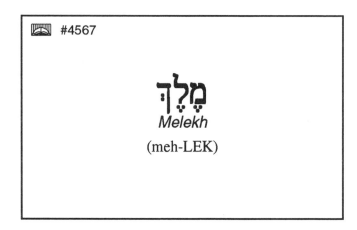

#4567

מֶלֶךְ

Melekh

(meh-LEK)

Melekh means "king" or "kingship." The bulk of the occurrences are in reference to a king of Israel (1 Samuel 2:10, for example). The first reference to a king is in Genesis 14:2ff. A war between nine kings is described, during which Lot, who chose to live in the city, was taken captive. Abram rescued his nephew, however, and afterward tithed of the spoils to Melchizedek, king of Salem. Salem (which means peace) is the old name for Jerusalem (the Jeru- prefix simply means "city of"). The Book of Hebrews tells us that Melchizedek was a type, or foreshadowing, of Jesus Christ.

Judges 9:8 is an unusual reference to a king in a parable of trees. Another rare usage of *melekh* is in Proverbs 30:27. Here, the sage notes that the wisdom of locusts who have no king, yet march in an organized rank.

The doctrinal importance of a king is seen in

Hosea 3:5. With David's appointment as king over Israel, a dynasty began that would never end. The king who would rule over the people of God forever, the promised Messiah, would come from the line of David. Hosea notes in 3:5 that in the last days, Israel will once again seek the LORD and David will be their king. This doesn't mean David, but the descendant of David. This future King is prophesied in God's promise to David concerning the eternal kingdom. The Messiah and King to come would be Jesus, born to Joseph and Mary by the miracle of a virgin birth. Jesus is the wise and righteous King Israel needs (Isaiah 32:1, Jeremiah 23:5).

Our sample verse is from Psalm 5:2. *Listen to my call for help, my* **King** *and my God, because it is to you I pray.*

#8747

תְּהִלָּה

T^ehillāh

(Te-HEEL-lah)

T^ehillāh means "praise the LORD." The English pronunciation is Hallelujah! Hallelujah means the same in every language of the world. *T^ehillāh* is the title of the Book of Psalms, a collection of praises and thanksgiving to God for who He is and for what He has done.

Praises to men are not to be on the same level as those to God. Those who fear the LORD first, however, are often honored, as was Daniel and Joseph, for example. Israel was to be exalted among the nations of the world, but they did not remain faithful to the LORD (Deut. 26:19).

Perhaps the greatest of all the Psalms are Psalm 120-134. Known as the Egyptian Hallels (short for hallelujahs), these Psalms tell of the deliverance of Israel from Egypt and are read at Passover time because the exodus represents leaving the land of sin to follow God. Exodus 15 records the original praise song led by Moses and his sister Miriam. Psalm 149:1 commands God's people to praise him. Reading the Psalms tells of the hundreds of acts of God's mercy and help to his people. A thorough reading relates many reasons for God's people to praise the LORD. Just thinking about God's blessings causes the believer to be thankful.

Our sample verse is from Psalm 150:6. *Let everything that has breath, praise the LORD.*

#5204

Nāvî'

(nah-VEE)

Nāvî' means "prophet" and is one of the three main offices of Old Testament Israel. (The other two are priest and king.) When thinking of a prophet, one usually thinks of Isaiah, Jeremiah or Jonah, etc. But there were other prophets in Old Testament times besides those who preached to Israel. Throughout the Old Testament, prophets were used by God to communicate his message to the people. The closest definition we have of prophet today is "preacher."

Noah was a prophet, because he warned people for 120 years of the coming judgment of the flood. Sadly, no more than seven others believed him. Abraham was also a prophet. The Scripture does not usually describes him in these terms, but in Genesis 20:7, God told King Abimelech that Abraham was a prophet and would pray for Abimelech's disease and he would be healed. We see from this account, and others in Abraham's life, that God spoke closely with Abraham, the patriarch of the coming nation.

Moses led the fully developed nation of Israel out of Egypt. At the end of Deuteronomy, it states that Moses was the closest to God as anyone had ever been from his time to the time Deuteronomy was written.

Deuteronomy 34:10 notes that God spoke with Moses "face to face." When Moses received the Law on Mt. Sinai, his life was miraculously sustained for 40 days. When he returned from the mountain, his face glowed, since he was near God's presence (Exo. 34:29-35).

True prophets always spoke the truth and did not conceal their identity. In most prophetical Books, the prophet notes who he is. Read Habakkuk 1:1 or Hagaii 1:1 for example. False prophets were also around. They weren't called false prophets because they lied all the time, but if they did not give a true prophecy any of the time! (Deut. 18:22). False prophets are those who try to sway people to follow some god other than Yahweh. (See Jer. 2:26, 8:1, 10; 1 Kings 22 and Isa. 9:14 for examples.) But God's prophets were faithful, even in the face of opposition (Hosea 6:5). Jeremiah preached over 50 years. Even though no one believed his message, he was doing what was right, because he was obeying God.

The greatest of all prophets was John the Baptist (Matt. 11:7-15). The accounts of John the Baptist are found in the New Testament, but he actually lived in the Old and New Testament time periods. He was born 6 months before Jesus (his first cousin by earth standards) and was the one chosen to point out the Messiah to Israel. All the prophets foretold that a Messiah would come, but only one actually saw Him.

Our sample verse is from 2 Kings 9:7. *This is what the LORD, the God of Israel says, "I will avenge the blood of my servants the* **prophets.** *"*

📖 #5177

נְאֻם
Nā'um
(Nah-OOM)

Nā'um is a special prophetical term which means "a declaration" or "sure saying." It can also have a simple meaning of "oracle" as in Balaam's oracles (Num. 24:3). But usually this phrase is only used by prophets who were called by God to give a special message to the people of Israel. The only prophetical Books which do not contain *nā'um* are Habakkuk, which is a record of questions to God and his answers, and Jonah, which is more about the story of the prophet learning a lesson than his message.

The prophet would preach his message and every once in a while he would say *nā'um*. This is somewhat related to our word "amen" which, interestingly enough, comes from the Greek word for amen, which in turn comes from the Hebrew word for amen. The meaning has remained the same for "amen" throughout the centuries. Today, someone might say amen during a sermon which means, "Yes, that's right." The original meaning is "surely" or "truly."

Nā'um, however, is much stronger, because it is followed by God's name. (See Zechariah 8:17, for example.) Rather than a simple human consent, *nā'um* means that God has spoken what is being said. From this we understand that *nā'um* was not spoken rashly or frivolously. The prophet was in earnest when he ended a section of his sermon by using this Hebrew word and was letting the people know he wasn't just giving his opinion. Sometimes the word was even repeated twice for double emphasis (Isa. 14:22). Repeating *nā'um* also indicated the surety of the prophecy.

The question is often asked, "How could one prophecy be more sure than another when they all come from God?" The answer is, some prophecies were spoken as warnings to sinful people. If the people repented, the judgment was averted. A good example of this is the judgments prophesied against Ninevah. When Jonah preached, Ninevah repented and God spared them. When Nahum warned the same city years later, the people didn't listen and the city was destroyed.

Another Hebrew principle enters in with the use of *nā'um*. When preaching, the prophets often used the *perfect* form of the actions which they were foretelling. In Hebrew, the perfect form of the verb means the action has already happened. The reason for prophesying future events with past tense verbs indicated that when the True God said something, it was as good as done.

Our sample verse is from Zechariah 13:2. *"On that day,"* [**a declaration** *of the* Lord,*] "I will banish the names of the idols from the land and they will not be remembered any more."*

#5081

מָשִׁיחַ

Māshîach

(mah-SHEE-ak)

Māshîach means "Messiah" or "deliverer." The literal meaning is "anointed one." For this reason, the term could refer to an ordinary man, but most often refers to the One coming to deliver the nation of Israel from sin.

The priests were anointed for special tasks (Lev. 4:3). Some were to make sacrifices, others took care of the tabernacle when it had to be moved. Still others took care of all the instruments and furniture. Only a few had the important task of moving the Ark of the Covenant. Priests with this duty had to be very careful to follow the exact instructions or be struck dead.

Saul was anointed to be king by the prophet Samuel. As such, David would not kill Saul even though Saul had tried to kill David many times. 1 Samuel 24:5-7 records David's opportunity. Instead of killing Saul, David simply cut off a corner of Saul's robe. David told his men that it would be wrong to do harm to one who was anointed of the LORD. Whatever Saul was guilty of was not the question; it was simply that he was still the king.

The Book of Judges tells of many deliverers who rose up for the nation of Israel. Samson was no doubt the most famous. One special messiah or deliverer in

Old Testament times, though, wasn't even an Israelite. Isaiah 45:1 prophesies of Cyrus, the foreign king.
Cyrus gave the order to allow the Jews to return to
Israel. Daniel gives a further prophecy concerning
this issue. From the time Cyrus gave the order for the
return of Israelite to their homeland to rebuild it, until
the time the Anointed One comes and is cut off (a
term sometimes meaning "to reject"), 69 weeks would
pass. Now a week in Hebrew was seven time periods. One week was usually seven days or seven years
just as Jacob worked a week, or seven years, for each
of his brides (Gen. 29:27). Multiplying 69 and 7 yields
483 years. History tells us that exactly 483 years
passed between the decree of Cyrus and the rejection
and crucifixion of Jesus. (Daniel prophesied a 70th
week, which is the Great Tribulation.)

The Psalms often speak of the greatest Messiah.
Jesus Christ (Christ is the Greek version of Messiah)
is the Messiah that the entire Old Testament points to.
Isaiah 61:1, 2 records the mission of the Messiah.
Jesus quoted these verses in reference to himself. The
Psalms also give many prophecies concerning the
Messiah. Psalm 22 is a famous one. Psalm 118 is the
one Jesus and his disciples sang on the night of the
last supper. Look up these Psalms as well as 2:2, 89:33
and 132:10, 17, 22.

Our sample verse is from Psalm 132:17. *I will make
a horn grow for David; I will put a lamp for my*
Anointed One.

▨ #8086

שְׁאֵרִית

Shᵉ'arîth

(sheh-ah-REETH)

Shᵉ'arîth is a typical example of amazing Hebrew words. It is quite ordinary in its normal usage, but takes on great theological significance when used in special ways. *Shᵉ'arîth* means "what is left over," "the remainder" or more specifically "the remnant."

An ordinary usage of *shᵉ'arîth* is found in 1 Chron. 12:39 where it speaks of the final triumph of David over Saul. When it was known that David was to be crowned king in Hebron, "all the rest" of Israel, besides the ones at Hebron, were agreed that it should be so. While a remnant of Israel was always around, Zephaniah 1:4 prophesies that the remnant of the false prophets of Baal would be completely cut off. The prophets warned Israel that if they continued their bent on evil and their serving of foreign gods, that another nation would come to destroy them and carry the Israelites off to a foreign land (Amos 5:5). Several years later, Jeremiah sadly noted that the last remnant of people were taken away into captivity (Jer. 41:10).

But other prophesies tell of another remnant, the

remnant that would return to the promised land and become a nation again. Micah 5:7, 8 foretells that Israel will once again become a great nation in the midst of other nations. Even Assyria, the very nation that once destroyed Israel's territory and captured her people, would not be able to conquer the mighty nation of Israel, because the Israelites had once again turned to God. The good thing about the 70 captivity years is that Israel turned away from their idolatry for good.

Remnant is a favorite theme of Isaiah and can be found in Isaiah 10:20, 11:11, 37:4, just to name a few of the many references. All prophets promised a restoration if people would repent, and nearly all prophesied of the remnant of Israel. The remnant indicates God's faithfulness to his covenants and the promise of things to come. No matter how evil the nation of Israel became there were always those who remained faithful to the LORD.

As is often said, the Old Testament points forward to the New. When reading the prophets and studying the themes therein, this becomes even more clear. Today, the people of God are the Christians around the world. In the centuries after Christ walked the earth, nations have tried to stamp out the Word of God and Christianity, but God has always been faithful to preserve a people of his name.

Our sample verse is from Jeremiah 6:9. *The LORD of hosts says, "Let them gather the **remnant** of Israel."*

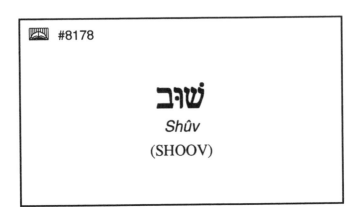

#8178

שׁוּב

Shûv

(SHOOV)

Shûv is a Hebrew verb which can have many meanings depending on the context. The usual meanings include "to turn aside," "to turn back" and "to return." Ordinary uses of *shûv* occurs hundreds of times in the Old Testament (e.g. 2 Kings 8:3). In Ruth 1:16, Ruth told her mother-in-law, "Do not urge me to go back." In faith, Ruth went with her mother-in-law, married Boaz, and became the ancestress of King David.

The most significant usages of *shûv*, however, are in the records of the return of Israel to God and their physical return to the promised land of Canaan. It may, in fact, be accurately said that the consummation of Old Testament theology can be thought of in the concept of "return." The return to God symbolized, and resulted in, Israel's return from captivity.

The Old Testament account is one of: beginnings; the story of Abraham who was called from the land of Chaldees to go to a land God would later reveal to him; the entering of the Israelites into Egypt only to make a great Exodus from that land 2 million strong; the conquering power of the Israelite nation as long as they obeyed God; the sad upheaval of that nation as they turned to idolatry despite God's repeated warnings; and the return of the nation after their idolatry was cured. In all of these episodes, the theology of land-blessing is the theme, and the return to both is the culmination.

The remnant that returned from Babylon carried forth the original mission of Israel, which was to be a nation who would go forth in the name of the LORD and be a witness to the nations of the One True God.

Ezra 6:19-22 tells of the celebration of the Passover feast after the return from Babylon. The Levites purified themselves, slaughtered the Passover lamb, and ate together. They celebrated 7 days and were filled with the joy of the LORD who had changed the heart of the Assyrian king. Nehemiah 8:17 tells of the celebration of the feast of tabernacles after returning. Symbolizing Israel's Exodus from Egypt, the land of sin, and their journey to Canaan, the feast of tabernacles shows the temporary dwelling of God's people until the promised land, representing heaven, was reached. Throughout the Scripture, the call to everyone is to return to the LORD.

Our sample verse is the final verse of the Old Testament, Malachi 4:6. *He will* **turn back** *the hearts of the fathers to the children, and the hearts of the children he will* **turn back** *to the fathers.*

A FINAL WORD

Now its time for you to discover the secret of why these 30 Hebrew words are so amazing. Because you learned them, you now possess the building blocks for a deeper understanding of the Old Testament. You may have noticed that the words were in a biblically ordered sequence.

With *30 Amazing Hebrew Words,* you have discovered the most basic Old Testament truths. **Yahweh, God** of everything, **created** the **heavens** and the **earth**. His **Spirit** made all living beings including **humankind** who **sinned** against Yahweh and **blood** had to be shed.

Yahweh made a **covenant** with Abraham stating that his **seed** would bless the world. Yahweh's **steadfast love** upheld that covenant, and Abraham fathered a **son** after Yahweh **intervened** concerning Sarah.

Burnt offerings were offered up to Yahweh in worship during Old Testament times as Yahweh was faithful to build the **household** of Abraham, Isaac and Israel, including King David. The Israelites were **to inherit** the land of Canaan and become a great **nation**. They set out to do this on the night of the **Passover**. During their journey, they received the **Law,** specifications for **priests** and an **ark** which would testify of Yahweh's presence among them and make provision for the Israelites **to atone** for their sin.

Although Yahweh was to be their **king**, Israel later requested a human king. They **sang praises** to

Yahweh as He gave them victories over their enemies. Soon, however, they turned away from Yahweh and began to serve other gods. **Prophets** were sent to warn them, but they didn't listen even though the prophets had a **declaration** from Yahweh. The prophets also foretold a **Messiah** who would deliver the people from their sins. After 70 years in captivity, a **remnant**, whom Yahweh had faithfully preserved **returned** to the promised land and once again began to seek the LORD.

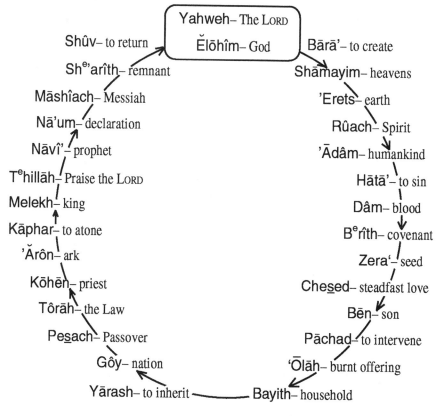

Use *30 Amazing Hebrew Words* with
Any Good Bible Study or Reference Tool

To get the most out of *30 Amazing Hebrew Words*, use it with any other Bible study tool. The best companion resource this author can recommend is a remarkable new Bible study tool called **The Complete Biblical Library** available from the publisher of this book, World Library Press, Inc.

The Complete Biblical Library offers a powerful study on every book, chapter, verse, and word in the Bible. The 16-volume New Testament work is complete, and a 20-volume Old Testament set is now in production. A new volume is being printed every three months. This amazing Bible study tool has been acclaimed by some of today's leading Bible scholars as the most useful of this century. **The Complete Biblical Library** lays open the Scriptures to any curious Bible student in an understandable and easy-to-use way. Anyone can study from the ground text quickly and accurately, without any previous knowledge of Greek or Hebrew.

World Library Press has made **The Complete Biblical Library** affordable to everyone through a simple plan. For more information on **The Complete Biblical Library** call World Library Press weekdays, 8-5 CT, Toll-Free, at **1-800-446-6238** Ext. V53.

Or write to: **World Library Press**
2274 East Sunshine Street • Dept. V5C
Springfield, Missouri   65804